JOEL SADLER-PUCKERING

# FERAL
# ANIMALS

Published in 2018

Hidden Voice Publishing

www.hiddenvoicepublishing.co.uk

Cover Illustration by Floyd

Cover Design by Grant Whitaker and Floyd

"I used to think I was ugly. I thought I looked like a camel. A person who doesn't love themselves, they will see anything that pops up on their face. I've seen squirrels, I've seen a bird and I've seen all kinds of animals on my face. But that is a result of self-hate." Mary J. Blige.

Dedicated to anyone who has ever seen an animal pop up on their face…

# CONTENTS

## FERAL ANIMALS

# FERAL ANIMALS

# FERAL ANIMALS: FOREWORD

Humans. What are we if we are not animals? We are instinctive creatures, driven by impulse, desire and a need to belong. Thrust into the world, kicking and screaming, we are moulded by our habitats as we navigate the structures of our environment and seek to live in wonder. Sometimes, however, this life feels like survival of the fittest and, just like in the animal kingdom, some of us will seek to push others down to rise to the top and be in control of our ideological spaces.

Sometimes we roam free and feral; sometimes we live in the cages we build in our minds. Sometimes all we want is to protect those we love; sometimes we seek to protect only ourselves.

When we are alone or seeking to be free, do we consider what the animal within us craves the most?

If humans are 'Feral Animals', consider this a wildlife study. Moments. People. Habitats.

We are at large.

We roam free.

We are brilliant.

# DEMONS

They created a furore and a fuss
with marches and protests.
When the winds of change
began to blow in swirls,
they manifested as plumes
of multi-coloured petals:
blood reds
envious greens
and dreamlike blues
pushed out the sallow, cream homogeny.

As the dust cleared, youngsters
waited with optimistic hope
for the clarity and acceptance
that the colour revolution promised.

But from the darkness came demons…
shapeless shadows
with narrow eyes
and crimson lips
that prepared
to give freedom a kiss of death.

## MAN FETUS

He begins coiled, cushioned, protected
in the warm and comfort of the womb.
Curled up and sheltered,
nourished and loved.
He will never know safety
and stability like this again.

Suddenly he is thrust out: brought to life.
Gripped hard, burdened by religion and
with the weight of heavy expectation
pushing down on his very being.

The nourishing comfort he once knew
has been ripped from him.

Unprepared for manhood,
he curls up
coils back
into his cushion
and protects only himself.

# BABY ON BOARD

Northern Line. London summer.
She breezes onto the
penultimate carriage and perches.
Floral print dress.
Generic flowers on black.
Her denim jacket neatly hides
the barely visible bump
she carries with pride.

Pinned to her lapel is a pin badge.
It adorns her. Draws attention.
Vastly visible to all:

*'Baby on Board'*

Protection.
Warning.
She hopes the words
will search.
Find the humanity
in this heartless world.
Stop the savage crowds from
pushing
shoving
trampling
her and her unborn child.

# BEAR HUNTER

A large stuffed teddy bear
rests peacefully
in a shopping trolley
in Asda Trafford Park.

He is a pacifist.
Stuffed. Loving.
Made for the cuddles.

Soon comes his nemesis…

7 years old. Adidas three-stripe.
Suspiciously surveying the enemy.
Hunting the bear. Ready for a fight.

He chops, kicks, punches.
No retaliation.
He chops, kicks, punches again.
Until he feels the bear is tame.

# MANCUB

Conceived in haste
but arriving with
hopes and aspirations
of new beginnings.
Immortalised as a picture:
a toothless smile
large ginger head
beaming like sunlight
in the middle of a collage
of grandchildren.

Familiar but distant.

Gushing first person
Facebook messages
on your birthday
from aunts and
Wythenshawe heads
using personal pronouns
even though you are too young to read.

A belated birthday
on 'family day'
where your father warns you
that you'll end up like him if
carry on getting into trouble at school.
SEN. A diagnosis.
Stories of how you can't sit still
and how you don't do as you are told
and how you ask constant questions
to gain attention but it comes to you in all the wrong ways.

Socially and educationally excluded,
you were last seen when you were twelve
by your second aunty
riding around the estate
on a stolen BMX bike
asking strangers for 20p
so you could buy chips for your tea.

You'll turn up again
as you always do.
Next time

I hope someone
pays you…attention.

# EMOTIONAL TERRORIST

Your heart has been radicalised
by the thirst for material satisfaction
and the desire to protect yourself
and your offspring from
the perceived dangers
of other people's opinion.

You have retreated into yourself
believing that only your
beliefs are correct
and that you are the only
one that might ever feel pain.

You have built misguided walls
to keep out the cruel, cruel world
and hid yourself from any
other outside love that you think
no longer understands you.

You have caused widespread devastation
with your words of mass destruction.

Your actions have caught
civilians with the ricochet
in this emotional war of terror.

# MENSWEAR

Shopping in December
in Manchester Arndale
is no place for the everyday male.

After navigating the jungle
of gender specific gifts:
golf balls
beer glasses
car related tat…
I was confronted by the
declaration of the 'muscle fit' shirt.

Manhood already dented by
my indifference to
golf balls and beer glasses,
my Pride was wounded when
a medium 'muscle fit' shirt
presented a mirror image
of a sub-masculine sausage.

Luckily, I was not alone
in my plight - a livid voice
from the next cubical loudly
expressed equal dissatisfaction
with his own 'muscle fit' garment.

'It's too tight' he hollered, exasperated.

'It makes me look gay.'

# LOVE BIRDS

She wrapped tightly
in oversized scarf
protecting her from
the cold and hostile world.

He covered and hidden
beneath baggy black hoodie
to keep him warm
as winter gives
its final sharp sting.

She with loose curls
gently thrown back
which would look fragile
and feather-light
if allowed to blow free in the wind.

He with unkempt clump
band t-shirt
and memories
of hedonistic evenings, in the fresh air
when the music touched his soul

Both a little scared
neither one prepared

... This is not a Disney movie

They share a glance
and a smile
but look away.

Headphones stay on
blocking their connection.

They head separately
to different destinations.
As far apart as strangers can be
in an urban carriage
where each soul uses technology
and tactical avoidance
to disconnect from
their dreams, humanity
and what might have been.

# HEN NIGHT

Expectations are up as the glitter comes down
Thick glossy make up paints over a frown
A pink, fluffy garter; tiara or crown
Army of eye lashes – the girls on the town

Clattering heels on the cold concrete cobbles
The one with the blisters, moving just at a hobble
An echoing holler: *'give your head a wobble'*
An angry reply leads to cat-fight or squabble

Destination: Canal Street. The hens make a splash
as they hit Via Fossa with oodles of cash
heading to the bar with an elbowing dash,
a pair of high heels and a 'bride to be' sash

A star of the night in a tight fitting dress
thinks *'it's a waste'* 'cos the guys aren't impressed
Her mate round the corner, wound up in a mess
vomit on her tits and hair stuck to her head

The end of the night - straight to Safads for food
some pushing and shoving: the punters are rude
'Be as quick as we can', the gaggle conclude
'cos the bride is outside and divorcing her shoes

# STAG NIGHT

As hen nights clatter by with balloons and
feral hedonism engulfs the street,
in crowded basements
behind tinted windows
the stags stomp, proud and powerful
baring their chests and huge antlers.

Locking horns
Following animal instinct
Sharing fixed glares
and impulsive movements.

The throb of the deep basslines
sound anonymous from the outside
but behind the secret glass walls
the stags hear the call of the wild.

Lips. Thighs. Torsos. Eyes.
No camouflage. No disguise.

Blackened walls offer no reflection
so the stags behave without constraint
and charge uninhibited into the night.

# ADDICTION

Eat it
Drink it
Overthink it
Love it
Place
no-one
above it
Taste it
Feel it
Mass appeal it
Touch it
Grab it
Got to
Have it

Works like voodoo
Sees right through you
Does what you do

as you undo.

# SUGAR RUSH

I try periodically to go cold turkey
but the sweetness pulls me back in
or slips the poison into my
pre-packed savoury food.

I know the future is bleak when I
watch the young attach themselves
to straws that feed them a similar syrup
until they can't sit still.

They too are hooked.

# DIARY OF A DISCO BALL

In my dirty disco dance deception
I had a neon recollection...
I once fell in love with my own reflection,
had sex so pure I needed no protection.

Spreading isms and prisms across the floor,
I pounded the beat until my feet felt sore
and I heard my frantic soul implore (me)
To curb the desire to spin some more...

# INFLATABLE PENIS

Seven girls on the lash
awkward in high heels,
floral prints and jump suits.
Lost under makeup
self-conscious and stiff
passing two hilarious
inflatable penises between them
and waving them proudly in the air.
A song request comes on: Tinie Tempah.
The girls do as desired and
'Go low. Go low.'
Who are they to disobey?
Obediently, they thrust themselves
towards the floor and move
like spades scraping across dirt.

# MID-FIGHT SNACK

Canal Street. Manchester.
Revellers roam feral and free.
A bollard creates a pedestrian
haven for this human traffic.

Three women emerge from
the amber streetlight consumed
by conflict and over-brimming emotion.
Screaming and pointing and insults
fly between the two lovers.

The third provides her pal with moral support
through the offering up of
a half-eaten pizza slice
which she holds helpfully in mid-air
so her mate can take a huge bite.

She does not have to stop gesticulating
but she is fed. Energized. Supported.
Able to continue her urgent quarrel
for a good while longer.

# FERAL ANIMALS

Some folk move as if the world is their own
and all the space that stretches in front of them
is theirs to do with as they please.
The streets
landscapes
meadows
dusty plains
sprawling oceans
are theirs for the taking.

Their children run free and wild
and ride the back of the wind.

All achieved by privileged wings.

Then there are those of us that hide
and fill the gaps of the spaces in between.
Moving with an apologetic gait
through margins and isolated spaces
making room for ourselves
building caves of protection.

We know the world is not ours
and we have no desire to take it.

Sometimes they clatter into us

Incredulous, they stare and wonder
how we dare to get in their way.

# GUTTER PRESS

Spreading hate
about the welfare state
twisting the minds
that you penetrate.

Gay men. Minorities.
Silence their voices
with science and vocab
about lifestyle choices.

Slander and liable
No need for the truth
Twist it and mould it
Feed it to the youth

Owned by the richest
protecting themselves.
Capitalist voice box
protecting their wealth.

Criminalised narratives
about council estates.
Reducing the poor
and dividing with hate.

# SEX AND THE CITY

Suited, blood-stained bodies
in chambers of sin.
Consumed and overtaken
from gluttony within.

Sexploitation soaked up
from vast billboards.
Pretty people sell us
goods we can't afford.

# BLACK FRIDAY

The humans prepare
with bated breath…
Ready to clamber
and stampede and fight
and claw and grab at
flat-screen televisions
like *feral animals*
hungry to be fed
goods and commodities.

They queue for two days
outside the Adidas
and the Apple shops to
quench their thirst for branding.

Just across the city, others
queue for food banks, whilst
somebody somewhere splashes
a spare four hundred and fifty
million dollars on a painting of Jesus.

# INTERNET ANIMAL

Twenty years of marriage
were a cage for this
husband, father of four and
internet prowler.

The digital revolution
has freed him
to make dirty cyber footprints
all over the minds of
insecure women
that too dwell in the cages
of their own low self-esteem.

The new world of technology
has helped him to
unleash his desires
and let lust run wild
all over his mind.

Finally, he is ready to pounce.
Turn the darkest desires
beaming brightly into his brain
into real, lustrous actual action.

# SAUSAGE DOG

Woodchip wallpaper
painted over at least seven times.
Plywood, mass produced drawers with
plastic golden handles
tucked neatly away into each corner.
A decaying, discoloured ribbon
attached to drawstring light switch
that once helped you to shed light
on endless situations with ease.
Fabric coat hangers - solid and gentle.
Ceramic animals survey the scene
from the dusty windowsill:
the clumsy sausage dog and
the slightly shimmering kingfisher.
Both, along with everything else
covered in a thin layer of talcum powder.
If I close my eyes, I can still see you
smoking a last cheeky fag, getting caught,
dishing out tongue lashings twice daily
and lying fearfully at the end of your days.

# NEST EGG

He waited six decades to retire.
35 years of night shifts
doing manual, physical and
dirty work.

Not extravagant or a show off.
He would flutter some loose
change in Ladbrokes
and splash out on simple
bespoke jewellery for anniversaries.
He would save the rest, in earnest
as he waited for glorious retirement.

They planned their brighter days
on the road and free from the grind
driving into the distance
with the dog
and a flask of hot coffee
and each other.

Fate had a different plan.

Six months before the
endless nights would finish,
life finished. His finger nails
still dirty from his manual work.

His nest-egg unhatched.

# ANIMAL PRINTS AND DIAMONDS

Sat at the bus stop
opposite The Happy Man pub
a patchwork of colours
waits for the 105
to take her to the precinct
and feed her addiction
to prescription medication
and The National Lottery.

A mayoress in huge gold chains.
Brash animal prints adorn her.
The first two plastic diamonds
drip from her ears
like cheap champagne
catching the light from the tired sun
as it struggles to raise its
weary head over the estate
on this typical Mancunian morning.

The third diamond adorns her hand
oversized and decadent
equal parts lucky dip and 90s hip hop.
The redistributed sunlight
casts colour over her sallow complexion
which contrasts gleefully
with her faded ginger beehive
and vivid pink tights.
She is a myriad of clashes and collisions.

The fourth diamond is somewhere inside
and shines brightest
out of her face when she smiles
and remembers him.

It is always there.

If you look hard enough.

# SKINNED ANIMALS

Some day in the near future
they dressed the same, androgynous
in black. With punk ass haircuts,
and tailored animal skins.
They crawled the white padded walls
played video games
smashed up post-modern art
like it had no value
and danced identically
whilst professing to be
individual.

They hollered in pain
but we were all too blind
to hear their calls.

# HIDDEN VOICE PUBLISHING

Hidden Voice Publishing is an independent publishing resource centre that supports & represents authors from under-represented groups with publishing paperback and Amazon Kindle books.

# TITLES ON HIDDEN VOICE PUBLISHING

*I KNOW WHY THE GAY MAN DANCES*
*JOEL SADLER-PUCKERING*

*INKY BLACK WOMAN*
*MINA AIDOO*

*FERAL ANIMALS*
*JOEL SADLER-PUCKERING*

*HIDDEN VOICE 2018 ANTHOLOGY*
*VARIOUS AUTHORS*
*(OUT OCTOBER 2018)*

Printed in Great Britain
by Amazon

11363363R00031